THE NEXT CHAPTER AFTER THE LAST

The Next Chapter After The Last

A.W. TOZER

CHOSEN AND EDITED BY
HARRY VERPLOEGH

CHRISTIAN PUBLICATIONS
Camp Hill, Pennsylvania

Christian Publications
3825 Hartzdale Drive, Camp Hill, PA 17011

The mark of 🕆 vibrant faith

ISBN: 0-87509-391-4
LOC Catalog Card Number: 87-70164
© 1987 by Christian Publications
All rights reserved
Printed in the United States of America

Cover photo by Mike Saunier

CONTENTS

FOREWORD

SINCE 1955 CHRISTIAN PUBLICATIONS has published seven collections of editorials written by A.W. Tozer. From 1950 until 1963, A.W. Tozer served as editor of *Alliance Life* (formerly *The Alliance Witness*), the official magazine of The Christian and Missionary Alliance. As compiler of this eighth anthology of his editorials, I am confident that these brief, eloquent affirmations of Christian orthodoxy — and their discerning criticism of the institutions responsible for the perpetuation of that heritage in this century — will continue to find thoughtful readers.

I have chosen the Easter editorial for March 17, 1951, to head my new selection because it demonstrates that though Tozer was often caustic in his commentary on the state of the North American Protestant church, he balanced his prophetic warnings with passionate affirmations of the Christian gospel. In "The Next Chapter after the Last," he celebrates the fact that those who chronicled the life of Jesus, including Luke in the Book of Acts, had to resume their biographies as chapters following the "final" account of a Life that for the first time in human record did not end "in a sepulchre at last." And because Christ "showed himself alive after his passion" (Acts 1:3), all His followers can expect to have another chapter. Seeing both the reality of death and the expectation of a resurrection which we affirm, Tozer wrote,

> How many saints since Bible times have lived and hoped and labored and worshiped, only to grow old and bent and to drop at last,

weak and helpless into the open grave. If that was for them the end, then we Christians would be of all men most miserable. But it was not the end. For all of God's true children there will be another chapter, a chapter that will begin with the resurrection and go on as long as eternity endures.

A.W. Tozer stands among the important Christian writers of our century who tried to find "enough paper and enough ink" to echo the good news of "the chapter which can have no ending." All his editorials published to date can be found in these volumes:

The Root of the Righteous (1955)
Born after Midnight (1959)
Of God and Men (1960)
That Incredible Christian (1964)
Man, the Dwelling Place of God (1966)
God Tells the Man Who Cares (1970)
The Set of the Sail (1986)
The Next Chapter after the Last (1987)

Harry Verploegh
Wheaton, Illnois
April 1987

The Next Chapter after the Last

THE FOUR GOSPELS tell the story of the life and ministry of Jesus, and in so doing, they follow accurately the ordinary course of biography, giving the facts of His birth, growth, work, death and burial. That is the way with biography: the very word itself suggests it, for it comes from *bios*, life, and *graphein*, to write, and means the written history of a person's life. So says Noah Webster.

Now, when we look at the Gospels we note an odd—and wonderful—thing. An extra chapter is added. Why?

Biography, by its own definition, must confine itself to the record of the life of an individual. That part of the book which deals with the family tree is not biography, but history, and that part which follows the record of the subject's death is not biography either. It may be appraisal, or eulogy, or criticism, but not biography, for the reason that the *"bios"* is gone: the subject is dead. The part that tells of his death is properly the last chapter.

The only place in world literature where this order is broken is in the four Gospels. They record the story of the man Jesus from birth to death, and end like every other book of biography has ended since the art of writing was invented. Matthew says, "And when Joseph had taken the body, he wrapped it in a clean linen cloth, and laid it in his own new tomb." Mark says, "And he [Joseph] bought fine linen, and took him [Jesus] down, and wrapped him in the linen, and laid him in a sepulchre which was hewn out of a rock." Luke writes, "And the women also, which came with him from Galilee, followed after, and beheld the sepulchre, and how his body was laid." John says, ". . . There was a garden; and in the garden a new sepulchre, . . . There laid they Jesus." They all agree: Jesus was dead. The life about which they had been writing was gone. The biography was ended.

Then, for the only time in this history of human thought, a biographer adds to his book a new section which is authentic biography and begins to write a chapter to follow the last chapter. This time the story did not end with a funeral. The Subject, whose story should have ended at death, was once again back among men to challenge new writers to try to find enough paper and enough ink to write the rest of the story of the life that can never end. Whatever is written of Him now is written of a living man. He was dead, but He is alive forevermore.

That such a thing could be was intimated by the miracles of restoration which our Lord performed during His earthly ministry. The widow's son was brought back to life for a brief time; at our Lord's gentle call Jairus's little daughter rose from her bed of death; and Lazarus, at Christ's command, came forth bound hand and foot. These were but vague disclosures of what was to come, and were at best only temporary suspensions of the inexorable law which demands that death shall always follow life—death complete and final. For these all died again, and the rule of biography was upheld. Each ended in a sepulcher at last. And that sepulcher was the period at the end of the last chapter.

What a perpetual wonder it is, then, that the biography of Jesus had to be resumed. Luke added not merely another chapter, but a whole book. The Book of Acts was a logical necessity. "He showed himself alive after his passion," writes Luke. The rest of the New Testament gives us some idea of what He is doing now, and prophecy reveals a little of what He will be doing through the ages to come.

That next chapter after the last is the source of all the Christian's hope, for it assures us that our Lord has put death in its place and has delivered us from the ancient curse. Death did not end the activities of our Lord; it did not even interrupt them, for while His body lay in Joseph's new tomb, He was preaching to the spirits in prison (1 Peter 3:18–20). And after three days, His spirit was reunited with His body and the new chapter began, the chapter which can have no ending.

Had Christ not risen from the dead, His life, beautiful as it was, would have been a human tragedy. Since He did in fact rise, His life has been shown to be an unrelieved triumph. The blood, the pain, the rejection, the agony of dying, the cold, stiff body and the colder tomb—these belong to the former days. The days that are now are days of hope and life and everlasting freedom.

What is true of Christ is true also of all who believe in Him. How many saints since New Testament times have lived and hoped and labored and worshiped, only to grow old and bent and to drop at last, weak and helpless, into the open grave. If that was for them the end, then we Christians would be of all men most miserable. But it was not the end. For all of God's true children there will be another chapter, a chapter that will begin with the resurrection and go on as long as eternity endures.

> *The powers of death have done their worst,*
> *But Christ their legions hath dispersed:*
> *Let shouts of holy joy outburst—*
>
> > *Alleluia!*
>
> *The three sad days have quickly sped;*
> *He rises glorious from the dead;*
> *All glory to our risen Head!*
>
> > *Alleluia!*
>
> *He brake the age-bound chains of hell;*
> *The bars from heaven's high portals fell;*
> *Let hymns of praise His triumph tell,—*
>
> > *Alleluia!*
>
> — MEDIEVAL LATIN

Quality versus Quantity

TIME MAY SHOW that one of the greatest weaknesses in our modern civilization has been the acceptance of quantity rather than quality as the goal after which to strive.

This is particularly evident in the United States. Costly buildings are constantly being erected with no expectation that they shall last more than one short generation. It is a common sight in our great cities to see workmen tearing down buildings which a few short years ago were considered the finest examples of the builder's art. So poor are our present materials and so fast do our modern tastes change, that there is even a kind of sad humor about the appearance of buildings erected more than 50 years ago.

Not only in our architecture but almost everywhere else is this psychology of impermanence found. A beauty salon ad recently defined a term which has long needed clarification. It read: "Permanent Waves. Guaranteed to last three months." So, permanence is the quality of lasting three months! These may be extreme cases, but they illustrate the transiency of men's hopes and the brevity of their dreams apart from God.

The church also is suffering from a left-handed

acceptance of this philosophy of impermanence. Christianity is resting under the blight of degraded values. And it all stems from a too-eager desire to impress, to gain fleeting attention, to appear well in comparison with some world-beater who happens for the time to have the ear or the eye of the public.

This is so foreign to the Scriptures that we wonder how Bible-loving Christians can be deceived by it. The Word of God ignores size and quantity and lays all its stress upon quality. Christ, more than any other man, was followed by the crowds, yet after giving them such help as they were able to receive, He quietly turned from them and deposited His enduring truths in the breasts of His chosen 12. He refused a quick shortcut to the throne and chose instead the long painful way of the cross. He rejected the offers of the multitude and rested His success upon those eternal qualities which He was able to plant in the hearts of a modest number of redeemed men. The ages have thanked God that He did.

Pastors and churches in our hectic times are harassed by the temptation to seek size at any cost and to secure by inflation what they cannot gain by legitimate growth. The mixed multitude cries for quantity and will not forgive a minister who insists upon solid values and permanence. Many a man of God is being subjected to cruel pressure by the ill-taught members of his flock who scorn his slow methods and demand quick results and a popular following regardless of quality. These children play in the marketplaces and cannot overlook the affront we do them by our refusal to dance when they whistle or to weep when they out of caprice pipe a sad tune. They are greedy for thrills, and since they dare no longer seek them in the theater, they demand to have them brought into the church.

We who follow Christ are men and women of eternity. We must put no confidence in the passing scenes of the disappearing world. We must resist every attempt of Satan to palm off upon us the values that belong to mortality. Nothing less than forever is long enough for us. We view with amused sadness the frenetic scramble of the world to gain a brief moment in the sun. "The book of the month," for instance, has a strange sound to one who has dwelt with God and taken his values from the Ancient of Days. "The man of the year" cannot impress those men and women who are making their plans for that long eternity when days and years have passed away and time is no more.

The church must claim again her ancient dowry of everlastingness. She must begin again to deal with ages and millenniums rather then with days and years. She must not count numbers but test foundations. She must work for permanence rather then for appearance. Her children must seek those enduring things that have been touched with immortality. The shallow brook of popular religion chatters on its nervous way and thinks the ocean too quiet and dull because it lies deep in its mighty bed and is unaffected by the latest shower.

Faith in one of its aspects moves mountains; in another it gives patience to see the promises afar off and to wait quietly for their fulfillment. Insistence upon an immediate answer to every request of the soul is an evidence of religious infantilism. It takes God longer to grow an oak than to grow an ear of popcorn.

It will cost something to walk slow in the parade of the ages while excited men of time rush about confusing motion with progress. But it will pay in the long run—and the true Christian is not much interested in anything short of that.

CHAPTER

3

We Must Stay by the Majors

IN LIFE THERE will be found certain great funda-
mentals, like pillars bearing up the weight of
some mighty building. These fortunately are kept
at a minimum in the total scheme of things. They
are not hard to discover: love, loyalty, integrity,
faith; these with a very few others constitute the
pillars upon which rests all the highly complex
superstructure.

The wise man will simplify his life by going to the
center of it. He will look well to the foundations
and, having done that, he will not worry about the
rest.

Life as we know it in our painfully intricate civilization can be deadly unless we learn to distinguish
the things that matter from those that do not. It is
never the major things that destroy us, but invari-
ably the multitude of trifling things which are mis-
takenly thought to be of major importance. These
are so many that, unless we get out from under
them, they will crush us body and soul. This is
becoming more and more evident as many of our
physical ills are being traced back to other than
physical causes. Doctors are becoming increasingly

aware of the deadly effects of the burden of the imponderables; they are learning that if they would do the patient any permanent good they must minister to the mind as well as to the body.

In the Christian life also we find this pattern repeated: a few important things and a world of burdensome but unimportant ones. The Spirit-taught Christian must look past the multiplicity of incidental things and find the few that really matter. And let it be repeated for our encouragement, they are few in number and surprisingly easy to identify. The Scriptures make perfectly clear what they are: the fact of God, the Person and work of Christ, faith and obedience, hope and love. These along with a few more constitute the essence of the truth which we must know and love. Christ summed up the moral law as love to God and man. Salvation He made to rest upon faith in God and in the One whom He had sent. Paul simplified the wonders of the spiritual life in the words, "Christ in you, the hope of glory."

The temptation to forget the few spiritual essentials and to go wandering off after unimportant things is very strong, especially to Christians of a certain curious type of mind. Such persons find the great majors of the faith of our fathers altogether too tame for them. Their souls loathe that light bread; their appetites crave the gamy tang of fresh-killed meat. They take great pride in their reputation as being mighty hunters before the Lord, and any time we look out we may see them returning from the chase with some new mystery hanging limply over their shoulder.

Usually the game they bring down is something

on which there is a biblical closed season. Some vague hint in the Scriptures, some obscure verse about which the translators disagree, some marginal note for which there is not much scholarly authority: these are their favorite meat. They are especially skillful at propounding notions which have never been a part of the Christian heritage of truth. Their enthusiasm mounts with the uncertainty of their position, and their dogmatism grows firmer in proportion to the mystery which surrounds their subject.

Dr. Samuel Johnson, the famous English sage, once said that one of the surest evidences of intellectual immaturity is the desire to startle people. Yet there are Christians who have been fed upon the odd, the strange and the curious so long and so exclusively that they have become wholly unfitted spiritually to receive or to appreciate sound doctrine. They live to be startled by something new or thrilled by something wonderful. They will believe anything so long as it is just a little away from the time-honored beliefs of sober Christian men. A serious discourse calling for repentance, humbleness of mind and holiness of life is impatiently dismissed as old-fashioned, dull and lacking in "audience appeal." Yet these things are just the ones that rank highest on the list of things we need to hear, and by them we shall all be judged in that great day of Christ.

A church fed on excitement is no New Testament church at all. The desire for surface stimulation is a sure mark of the fallen nature, the very thing Christ died to deliver us from. A curious crowd of baptized worldlings waiting each Sunday for the quasi-religious needle to give them a lift bears no relation whatsoever to a true assembly of Christian believers. And that its members protest their undying faith in the Bible does not change things any. "Not everyone that saith unto me, Lord, Lord, shall enter into the kingdom of heaven; but he that doeth the will of my Father which is in heaven."

Every believer as well as every minister of Christ must decide whether he will put his emphasis upon the majors or the minors. He must decide whether he will stay by the sober truths which constitute the beating heart of the Scriptures or turn his attention to those marginal doctrines which always bring division and which, at their best, could not help us much on our way to the Celestial City.

No man has any moral right to propound any teaching about which there is not full agreement among Bible Christians until he has made himself familiar with church history and with the development of Christian doctrine through the centuries. The historic approach is best. After we have discovered what holy men believed, what great reformers and saints taught, what the purest souls and mightiest workers held to be important for holy living and dying—then we are in a fair position to appraise our own teaching.

Humility is the only state of mind in which to approach the Scriptures. The Spirit will teach the humble soul those things that make for his salvation and for a holy walk and fruitful service here below. And little else matters.

CHAPTER

4

Complaining: A Disease of the Soul

AMONG THOSE SINS most exquisitely fitted to injure the soul and destroy the testimony, few can equal the sin of complaining. Yet the habit is so widespread that we hardly notice it among us.

The complaining heart never lacks for occasion. It can always find reason enough to be unhappy. The object of its censure may be almost anything: the weather, the church, the difficulties of the way, other Christians or even God Himself.

A complaining Christian puts himself in a position morally untenable. The simple logic of his professed discipleship is against him with an unanswerable argument. Its reasoning runs like this: First, he is a Christian because he chose to be. There are no conscripts in the army of God. He is, therefore, in the awkward position of complaining against the very conditions he brought himself into by his own free choice. Secondly, he can quit any time he desires. No Christian wears a chain on his leg. Yet he still continues on, grumbling as he goes, and for such conduct he has no defense.

The complainer is further embarrassed by the moral company in which he finds himself. His is a spiritual affinity with some pretty shady characters: Cain, Korah, the sulky elder brother, the petulant Jews of the Book of Malachi who answered every fatherly admonition of God with an ill-humored "Wherefore have we? Wherein have we?" These are but a few faces that stand out in the picture of the disgruntled followers of the religious way. And the complaining Christian, if he but looks closely, will see his own face peering out at him from the background.

Lastly, the believer who complains against the difficulties of the way proves that he has never felt or known the sorrows which broke over the head of Christ when He was here among men. After one look at Gethsemane or Calvary, the Christian can never again believe that his own path is a hard one. We dare not compare our trifling pains with the sublime passion endured for our salvation. Any comparison would itself be the supreme argument against our complaints, for what sorrow is like unto His?

After saying all this we are yet sure that no one can be reasoned out of the habit of complaining. That habit is more than a habit—it is a disease of the soul, and as such, it will never yield to mere logic. The only cure is cleansing in the blood of the Lamb.

The Duty of Opposing

THE NEARER WE draw to the heart of God the less taste we will have for controversy. The peace we know in God's bosom is so sweet that it is but natural that we want to keep it unbroken to enjoy as fully and as long as possible.

The Spirit-filled Christian is never a good fighter. He is at too many disadvantages. The enemy is always better at invective than he will allow himself to be. The devil has all the picturesque epithets, and his followers have no conscience about using them. The Christian is always more at home blessing than he is opposing. He is, moreover, much thinner-skinned than his adversaries. He shrinks from an angry countenance and draws back from bitter words. They are symbols of a world he has long ago forsaken for the quiet of the kingdom of God where love and good will prevail. All this is in his favor, for it marks him out as a man in whom there is no hate and who earnestly desires to live at peace with all men.

In spite of his sincere longing for peace, however, there will be times when he dare not allow himself to enjoy it. There are times when it is a sin to be at peace. There are circumstances when there is nothing to do but to stand up and vigorously oppose. To wink at iniquity for the sake of peace is not a proof of superior spirituality; it is rather a sign of a reprehensible timidity which dare not oppose sin for fear of the consequences. For it will cost us heavily to stand for the right when the wrong is in the majority, which is 100 percent of the time.

We have developed in recent times a peace-loving, soft-spoken, tame and harmless brand of Christian of whom the world has no fear and for whom it has little respect. We are careful, for instance, never to speak in public against any of the false cults lest we be thought intolerant. We fear to talk against the destructive sins of modern civilization for fear someone will brand us as bigoted and narrow. Little by little we have been forced off the hard earth into a religious cloud-land where we are permitted to wing our harmless way around, like swallows at sundown, saying nothing that might stir the ire of the sons of this world.

That Neo-Christianity, which seems for the time to be the most popular (and is certainly the most aggressive), is very careful not to oppose sin. It wins its crowds by amusing them and its converts by hiding from them the full implications of the Christian message. It carries on its projects after the ballyhoo methods of American business.

Well might we paraphrase Wordsworth and cry, "Elijah, thou shouldst be living at this hour; America has need of thee." We stand in desperate need of a few men like Elijah who will dare to face up to the brazen sinners who dictate our every way of life. Sin in the full proportions of a revolution or a plague has all but destroyed our civilization while church people have played like children in the marketplace.

What has happened to the spirit of the American Christian? Has our gold become dim? Have we lost the spirit of discernment till we can no longer recognize our captors? How much longer will we hide in caves while Ahab and Jezabel continue to pollute the temple and ravage the land? Surely we should give this some serious thought and prayer before it is too late—if indeed it is not too late already.

CHAPTER

6

Power Requires Separation

HISTORY SHOWS CLEARLY enough that true spirituality has never at any time been the possession of the masses. In any given period since the fall of the human race, only a few persons ever discerned the right way or walked in God's law.

God's truth has never been popular. Wherever Christianity becomes popular, it is not on its way to die—it has already died.

Popular Judaism slew the prophets and crucified Christ. Popular Christianity killed the Reformers, jailed the Quakers and drove John Wesley into the streets. When it comes to religion, the crowds are always wrong. At any time there are a few who see, and the rest are blinded. To stand by the truth of God against the current religious vogue is always unpopular and may be downright dangerous.

The historic church, while she was a hated minority group, had a moral power that made her terrible to evil and invincible before her foes. When the Roman masses, without change of heart, were made Christian by baptism, Christianity gained popularity and lost her spiritual glow. From there she went on to adopt the ways of Rome and to follow her pagan religions. The fish caught the fisherman, and what started out to be the conversion of

Rome became finally the conversion of the church. From that ignominious captivity, the church has never been fully delivered.

Christianity's scramble for popularity today is an unconscious acknowledgment of spiritual decline. Her eager fawning at the feet of the world's great is a grief to the Holy Spirit and an embarrassment to the sons of God. The lick-spittle attitude of popular Christian leaders toward the world's celebrities would make such men as Elijah or George Fox sick to the stomach.

Saving truth is a rare treasure, and not many in any generation possess it. No man ever found the way to God by asking the church member on his way to a social.

Lot was a popular believer. He sat in the gates of Sodom. But when trouble struck, he had to send quick for Abraham to get him out of the jam. And where did they find Abraham? Out on the hillside, far away from the fashionable crowds. It has always been so. For every Elijah there have always been 400 hundred popular prophets of Baal. For every Noah there is always a vast multitude who will not believe it is going to rain.

We are sent to bless the world, but never are we told to compromise with it. Our glory lies in a spiritual withdrawal from all that builds on dust. The bee finds no honey while crawling around the hive. Honey is in the flower far away where there is quiet and peace and the sun and the flowing stream; there the bee must go to find it. The Christian will find slim pickings where professed believers play and pray all in one breath. He may be compelled sometimes to travel alone or at least to go with the ostracized few. To belong to the despised minority may be the price he must pay for power. But power is cheap at any price.

7

The Right Direction Is Forward!

W<small>E HAVE LITTLE</small> sympathy for the psychology expressed in the various "Back To" movements among Christians today. Our direction is not back, but forward.

Few acts are as futile as sitting down and singing "Backward, turn backward, O Time, in thy flight." We cannot turn the clock back. We cannot bring back better days. And it is not necessary or desirable that we should.

If by means of some fantastic "time machine" one of us were permitted to go backward and visit some favorite period of the past, he would in all probability find the experience extremely disappointing. He would find himself a kind of anachronism, wholly out of place and thoroughly unhappy.

To each one it is given to occupy his own spot in history. He must, like David, do the will of God by serving his own generation. It is in his own day that he must meet God in satisfying encounter. 't is in his today, not in some pensive yesterday, that he must explore the riches of divine grace, do his allotted work and win his crown.

Psychologists attribute certain abnormal mental

conditions to an unconscious desire to escape the responsibilities of adult life by returning to the quiet and security of the prenatal state. Our habit of trying to recapture the spiritual glow of some better time by going backward creates a suspicion that we have lost the will to fight and are retiring to a safer spot behind the lines where we can sit down in peace to dream of armies defeated and battles won.

Today is our day. No one at any time has ever had any spiritual graces that we at this time cannot enjoy if we will meet the terms on which they are given. If these times are morally darker, they but provide a background against which we can shine the brighter. Our God is the God of today as well as of yesterday, and we may be sure that wherever our tomorrows may carry us, our faithful God will be with us as He was with Abraham and David and Paul.

Those great men did not need us then, and we cannot have them with us now. Amen. So be it. And God be praised. We cannot have them, but we can have that which is infinitely better—we can have their God and Father, and we can have their Savior, and we can have the same blessed Holy Spirit that made them great.

The normal Bible direction is not backward, it is always forward. Jacob returned to the altar, but in doing so he did not go back, he went forward. The Prodigal Son did not say, "I will go back"; he said, "I will arise and go to my father." From where he was, going to his father's house was a forward step in his moral activities. It represented no retreat, but a distinct advance over his previous conduct.

The will of God is always the proper goal for every one of us. Where God is must be the place of desire. Any motion toward God is a forward motion. Even repentance is not a retreat toward the past but a decided march into a more glorious future. Restitution is not a return to yesterday but a step into a blessed tomorrow.

There is such a thing as going backward in the spiritual life. There is such a thing as a retreat from a spiritual position once held by us as individual Christians. And there is such a thing as denominations and missionary societies making a wholesale withdrawal from ground once won at tremendous cost.

If we find that we have gone back, then we should immediately reverse the direction and again go forward. The great truths of superior spiritual experiences, of high levels of personal living, of rapturous communion with the Three Persons of the Godhead, of victory over the flesh, of the gifts and power of the Spirit: what has happened to these? Once they marked us out and made us peculiar. What about it today? These are fair questions and they demand an answer.

If candid self-examination reveals a departure from the green pastures where once our fathers grazed, what then? Let there be no wasting of time in a futile mooning over the past. Rather let us arise and go! Let us go forward to a new and better place in God. The land lies before us. Let us go in and take it.

On the Public Reading of the Scriptures

THE BIBLE IS the most important book in the world, and for Christians it is just about the only book—certainly the only book that should claim the place of honor in the public worship of God. We are, we trust, duly grateful for every good spiritual book written since the close of the New Testament canon. We do not undervalue the devotional book or the carefully prepared theological work, but when saints meet in communion there should be but one book, the Bible.

The place given to the Scriptures by the different churches may be learned from the very architecture of the building in which their congregations gather. The ritualistic church builds itself around the altar. Toward that altar all eyes are directed and around that altar various and sundry choirs are ranged, to chant or respond or sing as the occasion may demand.

The typical Protestant church is quite different. Its center of interest is the pulpit, and upon that pulpit rests a copy of the Bible printed in the language of the people. Preachers may come and preachers may go, but that old pulpit Bible remains. There it lies while generations pass, a source of light in the world's darkness, a fountain of pure water in the world's barren desert. And that minister is considered the best who can best expound its sweet mysteries. Lack of oratorical gifts will be forgiven if the man of God will but open the Book and give his hearers to eat of the heavenly manna.

Of course we of this generation cannot know by firsthand experience how the Word of God was read in other times. But it would be hard to conceive of our fathers having done a poorer job than we do when it comes to the public reading of the Scriptures. Most of us read the Scriptures so badly that a good performance draws attention by its rarity.

It could be argued that since everyone these days owns his own copy of the Scriptures, the need for the public reading of the Word is not as great as formerly. If that is true, then let us not bother to read the Scriptures at all in our churches. But if we are going to read the Word publicly, then it is incumbent upon us to read it well. A mumbled, badly articulated and unintelligent reading of the Sacred Scriptures will do more than we think to give the listeners the idea that the Word is not important.

We do not, however, concur in the belief that because the Word has attained such wide circulation we should not read it in our public meetings. We should by all means read it, and we should make the reading a memorable experience for those who hear.

Every man who is honored with the leadership of

public worship should learn to read well. And do not imagine that anyone who can read at all can read well. Even learned men break down here. We are all familiar with those public figures who can talk fluently on almost any subject but flunk out miserably when they try to quote the Scriptures. Reading the Bible well is something not picked up overnight.

To read the Bible well in public we must first love it. The voice, if it is free, unconsciously follows the emotional tone. Reverence cannot be simulated. No one who does not *feel* the deep solemnity of the Holy Word can properly express it. God will not allow His Book to become the plaything of the rhetorician. That is why we instinctively draw back from every simulated tone in the reading of the Scriptures. The radio announcer's artificial unction cannot hide the absence of the real thing. The man who stands to declaim the Scriptures like a schoolboy reciting a passage from Hamlet can only leave his hearers with a feeling of disappointment. They know they have been cheated, though most of them could not tell just how.

Again, to read the Bible well, one must know what the words mean and allow them to mean just that, without putting any *body English* on the passage to make it take a turn of meaning not found in the text. Probably the hardest part of learning to read well is eliminating ourselves. We read best when we get ourselves out of the transaction and let God talk through the imperfect medium of our voice.

The beginner should read aloud whole books of the Bible in the privacy of his own room. In that way he can learn to hear his own voice and will know how he sounds to others. Let him consult a pronouncing Bible to learn the correct pronunciations of the names and places of the Bible. Let him cultivate the habit of reading slowly and distinctly with the reverence and dignity proper to the subject matter.

Surely Protestants deserve a better sort of Scripture reading than they are now getting in our churches. And we who do the reading are the only ones who can give it to them.

The Spiritual Love of Jesus

THE WHOLE OF true religion can be summed up in the spiritual love of Jesus.

To love God and to love our neighbor was said by our Lord to be the fulfilling of the law and the prophets. All Christians believe that God reveals Himself as Christ; so the love of Jesus is in truth the love of God.

Love as experienced by human beings may be on either of two levels, the human or the divine. These are not the same. They differ not only in intensity and elevation but in kind.

Human love is undoubtedly the best thing left to the human race. Though it is often perverted and sometimes degraded, it is still Adam's best product, and without it, life on earth would be unendurable. Let us imagine what the world would be like if every trace of human love were suddenly removed. The heart recoils from the contemplation of such a horror. Without love, earth would not differ from hell except for the difference of location. Let us treasure what is left of love among the sons of men. It is not perfect, but it makes life bearable and even sweet here below.

But human love is not divine love and should never be confused with it. Among the sentimental religionists, the two are accepted as being the very same and no distinctions are made. This is a great moral blunder and one that leads to spiritual frustration and disappointment. If we are to think clearly and pray rightly, we must recognize the difference between love that is merely human and that other love which cometh down from above.

Charles Wesley knew the difference and made it clear in his famous lines:

> *Love divine, all loves excelling,*
> *Joy of heaven, to earth come down.*

Here all grades and degrees of human love are acknowledged, and the true love which comes down from heaven is placed above them as far as the heaven is above the earth. This is not only good poetry, it is good theology as well.

The human heart can love the human Jesus as it can love the human Lincoln, but the spiritual love of Jesus is something altogether different from and infinitely superior to the purest love the human heart can know. Indeed it is not possible to love Jesus rightly except by the Holy Spirit. Only the Third Person of the Trinity can love the Second Person in a manner pleasing to the Father. The spiritual love of Jesus is nothing else but the Spirit in us loving Christ the Eternal Son.

Christ, after the flesh, receives a great deal of fawning attention from the liberal and the modernist, but love that is not the outflow of the indwelling Holy Spirit is not true spiritual love and cannot be acceptable to God. We do Christ no honor when we do no more than to give Him the best of our human love. Even though we love Him better than we love any other man, still it is not enough if He merely wins first place in competition with Socrates or Walt Whitman. He is not rightly loved until He is loved as very God of very God, and the Spirit within us does the loving.

There is much in present-day gospel circles that illustrates the distinction we are pointing out. A great many loud protestations of love for Christ leave the discerning heart with the impression that they are but sounding brass and tinkling cymbals. Innumerable sweet love ballads are sung to Jesus by persons who have never known the inward illumination of the Holy Spirit or felt the shock that comes with a true sight of the sinful pollution of nature.

While the all-important distinction between the human and the spiritual love of Jesus is one that must be *discerned*, and one which can scarcely be *explained*, we yet venture to point out some marks which may distinguish the two.

Reverence, for one thing, will always be present in the heart of the one who loves Christ in the Spirit. The Spirit gives a holy solemnity to every thought of Jesus, so that it is psychologically impossible to think of the true Christ with humor or levity. Neither can there be any unbecoming familiarity. The Person of Christ precludes all such.

Then, self-abasement is always found in the heart that loves Jesus with true spiritual love. When Paul saw Jesus, he fell on his face. John fell down as dead, and every soul that ever saw and felt the terror and wonder of His glorious Presence, has known some such experience of self-abasement.

It is most important that we know whether our relation to Jesus is divine or human. It will pay us to find out now.

Our Christian Obligation to Care

WHETHER OR NOT the Christian should separate himself from the world is not open to debate. The question has been settled for him by the Sacred Scriptures, an authority from which there can be no appeal.

The New Testament is very plain: "They are not of the world," said our Lord, "even as I am not of the world." James wrote, "Ye adulterers and adulteresses, know ye not that the friendship of the world is enmity with God? Whosoever therefore will be a friend of the world is the enemy of God." John said, "Love not the world, neither the things that are in the world. If any man love the world, the love of the Father is not in him."

Such teaching as this would appear to be plain enough, and there should be no doubt about what is intended. But we must never underestimate the ability of the human mind to get itself lost on a paved highway in broad daylight. Some well-intentioned souls have managed to get themselves confused about their relation to the world and have sought to escape it by hiding from it. They read into the biblical command to separate from the world the idea of complete withdrawal from all human activities and seek peace of heart by cutting themselves off, as far as possible, from the great stream of human life and thought. And that is not good.

We human beings were made for each other, and what any of us is doing at any time cannot be a matter of indifference to the rest of us. On the human plane all men are brothers. The Son of Man never denied this sweet tie with humankind. Over a stubborn and sinful Jerusalem He frankly shed tears and, in the hour of death, prayed for men who were so blind as to nail their God on a tree. And Paul, who burned always to be like his Lord, wept over unbelieving Israel with an anguish that goaded him to an utterance so daring as to cause the ages to wonder: "I have great heaviness and continual sorrow in my heart. For I could wish that myself were accursed from Christ for my brethren, my kinsmen according to the flesh."

Peace of heart that is won by refusing to bear the common yoke of human sympathy is a peace unworthy of a Christian. To seek tranquility by stopping our ears to the cries of human pain is to make ourselves not Christians but a kind of degenerate stoic having no relation either to stoicism or Christianity.

We Christians should never try to escape from the burdens and woes of life among men. The hermit and the anchorite sound good in poetry, but stripped of their artificial romance, they are not good examples of what the followers of Christ should be. True peace comes not by a retreat from the world but by the overpowering presence of Christ in the heart. "Christ in you" is the answer to our cry for peace. The Salvation Army lassie distributing gospel literature in a saloon is a better example of the separated life than a prim and cold-faced saint who has long ago fled the world to take refuge in the barren caverns of her soul.

The testimony of the true follower of Christ might well be something like this: The world's pleasures and the world's treasures henceforth have no appeal for me. I reckon myself crucified to the world and the world crucified to me. But the multitudes that were so dear to Christ shall not be less dear to me. If I cannot prevent their moral suicide, I shall at least baptize them with my human tears. I want no blessing that I cannot share. I seek no spirituality that I must win at the cost of forgetting that men and women are lost and without hope. If in spite of all I can do they will sin against light and bring upon themselves the displeasure of a holy God, then I must not let them go their sad way unwept. I scorn a happiness that I must purchase with ignorance. I reject a heaven that I must enter by shutting my eyes to the sufferings of my fellow men. I choose a broken heart rather than any happiness that ignores the tragedy of human life and human death. Though I, through the grace of God in Christ, no longer lie under Adam's sin, I would still feel a bond of compassion for all of Adam's tragic race, and I am determined that I shall go down to the grave or up into God's heaven mourning for the lost and the perishing.

And thus and thus will I do as God enables me. Amen.

The Growing Movement toward World Union

A T FIRST GLANCE the picture of the whole family of mankind uniting in one great brotherhood looks good, very good indeed. That all men everywhere should some day clasp hands to form a worldwide circle of love and good will has been the dream of the centuries. Robert Burns wrote the ringing words,

> For a' that, and a' that,
> It's coming yet, for a' that,
> That man to man the world o'er
> Shall brothers be for a' that.

The first half of the 20th century has seen some noble attempts to unite the peoples of the world in one common bond. The League of Nations was one such effort. Woodrow Wilson believed so fervently in the brotherhood of man that he sought to bring the United States into the League, and it is said, died brokenhearted when he failed in his purpose. The present United Nations organization has the same thing in mind—to achieve a vast superbody that will unite the divided peoples of the earth in ties of peace and mutual understanding.

Undoubtedly there is much to be said for the one-world idea. So much, in fact, that anyone who expresses a doubt of its ultimate soundness automatically invites the charge that he is a throwback to the days of feudalism, a narrow chauvinist, a religious bigot and a churlish misanthropist. And it is not hard to see why people flare up so violently against the objector. They are sick in heart and weary of world confusion. They have had enough of "wars and rumours of wars." They have seen "nation rise against nation and kingdom against kingdom" too long, and they are sick of the whole thing. They yearn for a long peace that will relieve them and their children and grandchildren from the horrors and sufferings that war brings.

We confess we should like to go along with the modern movement toward world unity, and we might do it except for two considerations. One is that in their move toward unity, the nations are not being drawn together, they are being *driven* together and that which drives them is *fear*. The 60 nations of the UN do not love each other, they fear each other, and they fear the rest of the world. And if every nation in the world were finally included in one huge superstate, the tie that bound them would be the same — mutual distrust and hate. And human nature being what it is, and God being who He is, *nothing that rests upon fear can be permanent*.

It is only being realistic to state that the nations of the world are motivated by hate and fear. Even in the United Nations the members do not trust each other, much less love each other. They muddle along like gamblers, bluffing and concealing and taking every advantage of fear and self-interest among the members to gain desired ends.

While a few superior men dream of true brotherhood, the masses of mankind are filled with jealousy, envy, hate and greed. World leaders are too often motivated by lust for power or by the selfish desire to gain and hold high position. A few (those on our side!) are truly devoted to the welfare of mankind, but for the most part, kings, presidents, prime ministers and high dignitaries generally think little of the good of the people or the future of the world. Men are basically bad, and all the talk about universal brotherhood is simply eyewash. The orators are plain scared, or they are trying to sell us a bill of goods. And we won't buy.

The second reason for rejecting the doctrine of world brotherhood is that it is out of accord with the teaching of the Scriptures. Any unity that may be achieved among nations will be but a temporary thing, and will be exploited by the coming Antichrist to secure his evil ends. Teachers of prophecy do not agree on all details, but the consensus among them is that the world is to see the rise of a superman who will unite mankind (or at least a large part of it) and set himself up as the divinely appointed world ruler, and long-desired Fuehrer of the race. This will be the false christ who will rise and shine for a brief time before the second coming of the true Christ.

It is impossible within the confines of a few pages to quote the Scriptures bearing on this topic. But the Bible is there, and anyone interested may read for himself. It could be that the present wide movement toward world union is a harbinger of the new age. It would pay us to search the Scriptures. They are a sure word "whereunto ye do well that ye take heed, as unto a light that shineth in a dark place, until the day dawn, and the day star arise in your hearts."

CHAPTER

12

"I'm a Stranger Here Myself"

Many of us have had the experience of finding ourselves in a strange city looking for the post office or some other public building. We accost a friendly looking man on the street and inquire where the building is to be found. He looks up with an apologetic smile, shakes his head and replies, "I'm sorry. I can't help you. I'm a stranger here myself."

All of us at some time in our life become suddenly aware that we are in a strange place called the world. We do not remember coming here and we are not sure when or how we are going to leave. A score of pressing questions fill our minds. We must have the answers. Where did we come from? What are we? Why are we here? Where do we go next? What does God require of us? How can we find the heaven of peace? Such questions as these insist upon an answer. But we have no answer.

Then we approach someone who looks as if he might know. We eagerly put our question, but we get only a shake of the head and the usual, "I'm sorry. I'm a stranger here myself."

At first we are frightfully disappointed, for we

had hoped someone might know. There are the great stone buildings covered with ivy where the best brains of the world hold forth day after day. There are the great libraries piled with solemn books, each filled with learned words. But the desired answer is nowhere. A few attempt to direct us, but prove by their own bewilderment that they know as little as we do about the whole thing. The philosopher seeks, but never finds. The scientist searches, but finds no data to help us beyond the last hour and the narrow house and the shroud. The poet soars on stubby wings, but soon comes down again, tired and confused. Each one has the same answer: "I'm sorry. . . . I'm a stranger here myself."

That is the only honest answer. Others are sometimes given, but they are never valid answers. They spring out of pride or error or uncritical and wishful thinking, and they are not to be trusted. It is no good asking for information of another who is as ignorant as ourselves. We are all strangers in a strange world.

Is our state hopeless then? Is no answer to be had? Must we live in a world we do not understand and go out into a future of dark uncertainty? No, thank God, things are not as bad as that. There is an answer. We can find light. Our questions have been answered. "From a child," wrote Paul to Timothy, "thou hast known the holy scriptures, which are able to make thee wise unto salvation through faith which is in Christ Jesus. All scripture is given by inspiration of God, and is profitable for doctrine, for reproof, for correction, for instruction in righteousness."

It is the universal testimony of the saints of the ages that when the light of the Scriptures enters, the darkness of spiritual ignorance vanishes. God's Word giveth light. It has answer for every question that matters. The merely curious question it ignores, but every real inquiry made by the sincere heart is met with full light.

It is important that we search the Scriptures daily, and more important still that we approach them with faith and humility, bowing our hearts to their instructions and commands. Then through faith in Christ we cease to be strangers and become sons of God.

We Must Think Like Christians

THIS IS A CRITICAL moment in American affairs of state. Our country is seriously divided. Political and military giants are squaring off in a battle of words that may have consequences not only at home but throughout the whole world for years to come.

The issues that divide our leaders are so important that few Americans can remain neutral. Almost everyone has a pronounced opinion, and is sure he is right. That men equally wise and good take the opposite side does not seem to occur to any of us. Feeling is running high, and most of our thinking is being done with our emotions.

"Our American way of life" is a phrase constantly heard these days. It is a good phrase, and to many sincere and honest persons it means liberty of conscience, freedom of individual enterprise and the right to worship God after the dictates of our own conscience; it means the rule of law instead of the rule of tyrants; it means a minimum of interference from the state and a maximum of liberty for the individual citizen.

To millions of others, however, it means little

more than the right to sin to their heart's content
without molestation by the civil authorities. The
Constitution may be, as Gladstone said it was, the
noblest document ever struck off by the mind of
man. But we must remember that there are count-
less thousands of Americans who use it merely as a
place to hide when they are caught in some act of
iniquity.

Liberty as used by the American founding fathers
meant freedom to do good; many today conceive it
to mean freedom to do evil, and they work it for all
the traffic will bear.

One thing must be kept in mind: We Christians
are Christians first and everything else after that.
Our first allegiance is to the kingdom of God. Our
citizenship is in heaven. We are grateful for political
freedom. We thank God for democracy as a way of
life. But we never forget that we are sons of God
and citizens of another city whose builder and
maker is God.

For this reason, we must not identify the gospel
with any political system or make Christianity to be
synonymous with any form of government, however noble. Christ stands alone, above and outside
of every ideology devised by man. He does not join
any of our parties or take sides with any of our
great men except as they may come over on His
side and try to follow Him in righteousness and
true holiness. Then He is for them, but only as
individuals, never as leaders of some political fac-
tion.

The true Christian will be loyal to his country and
obedient to those in authority, but he will never fall
into the error of confusing his own national culture

with Christianity. Christianity is bigger than any country, loftier than any civilization, broader than any human ideology.

It may shock some people to be told that Christ is not an American. Nor was He a Jew merely. He was born of the seed of Abraham of the line of David, and His mother was a Jewess of the tribe of Judah. Still Christ is vastly more than a Jew. His dearest name for himself was "the Son of man." He came *through* the Jewish race, but he came *to* the human race. He is Everyman's countryman and Everyman's contemporary. He is building a kingdom of all nations and tribes and tongues and peoples. He has no favorites, "but in every nation he that feareth him, and worketh righteousness, is accepted with him."

Let us remember that the gospel is a divine thing. It receives no virtue from any of man's religions or philosophies. It came down to us out of heaven, a separate thing, like Peter's sheet, wholly on its own. It is something given of God. It operates in the individual heart wherever that heart may be found.

Any form of human government, however lofty, deals with the citizen only as long as he lives. At the graveside it bids him adieu. It may have made his journey a little easier, and, if so, all lovers of the human race will thank God for that. But in the cool earth, slaves and free men lie down together. Then what matter the talk and the turmoil? Who was right and who was wrong in this or that political squabble doesn't matter to the dead. Judgment and sin and heaven and hell are all that matter then.

So, let's keep cool, and let's think like Christians.

Christ will be standing upright, tall and immortal, after the tumult and the shouting dies and the captains and the kings lie stretched side by side, the "cause" that made them famous forgotten and their whole significance reduced to a paragraph in a history book.

On Going to God First

IT IS CHARACTERISTIC of human nature to turn to God only after every other avenue of help has been explored and been found useless. This is one of the many evils which sin has visited upon us—the bent to look everywhere for aid but in the right place, and if we do look in the right place, to look there last.

No one likes to think that he has been a second choice, but our patient Heavenly Father lies under the shadow of always being at least second, and often third or fifth or tenth choice. For most of us will have to confess that we sought God only after all else had failed. When one friend after another had rejected our pleas, we turned in despair to the God who never rejects anyone who comes to Him in sincerity and faith.

The old country woman "'lowed" that it was no use to pray in a crisis if you hadn't been in the habit of praying before. "For," said she, "God doesn't hear skeered prayers." There may be a certain logic about her reasoning, but her conclusion is all at variance with the facts and with the gentle ways of God with erring men. For since our fathers fell asleep, the kingdom of heaven has continued to receive "skeered" persons of all ages and condiions who found the world too much for them and who in their grief and despair sought help where help can indeed be found.

No one need feel ashamed if he has come to God as a last resort, especially if he has found the help he sought "in the bosom of his Father and his God." God has received a great army of such persons, and if He is satisfied, we should be. Billy Sunday once testified that he had been scared into the kingdom of God. "But," said he, "by the grace of God I'm not going to be scared out."

But be all this as true as it may be, still it is a bad habit for us as Christians to get into—the habit of trying everything before taking our problems to God. God should come first. If in our sinful ignorance we once knew no better, there is no reason for our continuing in the same rut now that we are children of the kingdom. It cheats us out of many a victory and leaves us for long periods in a state of perplexity and distress when we might be walking in freedom without a care in the world.

Going to God first will head off many a bad situation. A young man falls in love and without as much as a word of counsel from God plunges into marriage. A few years later he finds that he has made a bad mistake. Then he goes to God to seek a way out, and learns that he is too late. God will still help him even in such circumstances, but the sacred vows have been taken, and the die is cast. It would have been better to go to God first.

A businessman gets too busy to pray and becomes involved in unsound business transactions. When things begin to go to pieces for him, he turns hard to God and begs for deliverance. After a while, hurt and chastened and much the poorer for his experience, he gets back on his feet again. Then he has time to ask how it all happened, and the answer is easy. He did not go to God first. He received help, all right, but also he suffered losses that he never should have suffered if he had gone to God first.

These examples may serve to illustrate our point. The details will vary from one to another of us, but the principle always remains the same. Our chastenings come when we look somewhere else for help and neglect the one real source of all help and comfort. It's always best to go to God first.

The Christian's Obligation to Be Joyful

FAITH IS AT THE foundation of all Christian living, and because faith has to do with the character of God, it is safe from all vacillations of mood. A man may be believing soundly and effectively even when his mood is low, so low that he is hardly aware that he alive emotionally at all.

That is one thing, and it is good to know and still better to put in practice. But like every other truth, it has two sides. Our trouble today is that we tend to forget the other side, that is, that elevated spiritual mood is a tremendous aid to victorious living.

The relation of faith to mood may be stated by means of a number of metaphors: if faith is the tree, mood is the blossom; if faith is the flower, mood is the fragrance; if faith is the instrument, mood is the melody. And who will deny the vital place of the blossom, the fragrance and the music in human life?

Mood is a kind of mental weather. There is weather in which nothing will grow. The farmer knows the damage done by prolonged periods of cold, wet weather in the spring after the seed has been planted. Sometimes the seed will rot in the ground, requiring a new planting with all the loss and extra work this entails. Weather may be too hot, too cold, too dry, too wet to favor good crops, and the Christian's moods, in like manner, may be unfavorable to spiritual growth and fruitfulness. Christian service carried on during prolonged heaviness of heart may be as good as wasted.

George Mueller would not preach until his heart was happy in the grace of God; Jan Ruysbroeck would not write while his feelings were low, but would retire to a quiet place and wait on God till he felt the spirit of inspiration. It is well known that the elevated spirits of a group of Moravians convinced John Wesley of the reality of their religion and helped to bring him a short time later to a state of true conversion.

The Christian owes it to the world to be supernaturally joyful. In this day of universal apprehension when men's hearts are failing them for fear of those things that are coming upon the earth, we Christians are strategically placed to display a happiness that is not of this world and to exhibit a tranquillity that will be a little bit of heaven here below.

All this takes for granted that sin has been dealt with by sincere repentance and thorough amendment of life. It assumes that we are walking in the light of truth, for true joy cannot be artificially induced. The "keep smiling" school of applied psychology is not even remotely related to the true faith of Christ. The chief fun of the comedian and the good humor of the wit who is the life of the party are like flowers growing on old graves, briefly interesting, but evanescent and always touched with sadness. But the fountain of Christian joy flows out from the throne of God, pure, refreshing and sweet everlastingly.

CHAPTER

16

"It Seemed Good in Thy Sight"

A DETERMINATION TO know what cannot be known always works harm to the Christian heart.

Ignorance in matters on our human level is never to be excused if there has been opportunity to correct it. But there are matters which are obviously "too high for us." These we should meet in trusting faith and say as Jesus said, "Even so, Father: for so it seemed good in thy sight."

There are things that we can never understand until we have the benefit of advanced experience and the addition of a light beyond anything we possess at present. Under those circumstances it is not good to attempt to understand. Confessed ignorance becomes us better.

Human curiosity and pride often combine to drive us to try to understand acts of God which are plainly outside the field of human understanding. We dislike to admit that we do not know what is going on, so we torture our minds trying to fathom the mysterious ways of the Omniscient One. It's hard to conceive of a more fruitless task.

For instance, a child which had been long desired

and prayed for is suddenly taken away. The parents are prostrated with grief, and to add to their suffering comes the torturing thought that they should know why it all happened, but do not. Then begins the long, painful attempt to learn the secret of life and death. Why did this happen? What does God have in mind? These poor friends bruise their minds cruelly trying to fathom the unfathomable.

Under such circumstances the Christian thing to do is to say, "That thou mightest be justified when thou speakest, and be clear when thou judgest . . . Even so, Father: for so it seemed good in thy sight." A blind confidence which trusts without seeing is far dearer to God than any fancied knowledge that can explain everything.

We may as well learn (and the earlier the better) that God has no private secretaries who are on the inside of the secrets of eternity. All God wanted to say, He has said in the Scriptures. Beyond that we show the greatest wisdom simply to remain still before Him and whisper, "Even so, Father." To the adoring heart, the best and most satisfying explanation for anything always will be, "It seemed good in thy sight."

Co-workers, Not Competitors

IT IS TOO BAD that anything so obvious should need to be said at this late date, but from all appearances, we Christians have about forgotten the lesson so carefully taught by Paul: God's servants are not to be competitors, but co-workers.

In any religious work there are two interests, either of which may be served: the spiritual interest or the natural; the divine or the human; our own or God's. And it is altogether possible to serve our own interests with poured-out devotion. It is possible to serve the flesh even while engaged in the most intense sort of religious activities. The very fact that our activities are religious will sometimes disguise the presence of the rankest kind of selfishness.

It is impossible for two servants of Christ to compete as long as the work they are doing is God's work. When the spirit of competition enters, we may be sure that the work of God is no longer being done. God is one; it is wholly impossible for Him to compete with Himself. As long as His Spirit is in control there can be no such thing as competition among those who are under that control. The

Spirit achieves cooperation, always, and makes of His servants not competitors, but co-workers.

A local church, as long as it is indwelt by the Holy Spirit, cannot entertain the psychology of competition. When it begins to compete with another church, it is a true church of God no longer; it has voided its character and gone down onto a lower level. The Spirit that indwells it is no longer divine; it is human merely, and its activities are pitched on the plane of the natural.

Wherever the spirit of competition between brethren rears its head, there will be found carnality, selfishness and sin. The only way to deal with it is to tag it for what it is and put it away in the sorrows of repentance.

The Holy Spirit always cooperates with Himself in His members. The Spirit-directed body does not tear itself apart by competition. The ambitions of the various members are submerged in the glory of the Head, and whatever brings honor to the Head meets with the most eager approval of the members.

We should cultivate the idea that we are co-workers rather than competitors. We should ask God to give us the psychology of cooperation. We should learn to think of ourselves as being members in particular of one and the same body, and we should reject with indignation every suggestion of the enemy designed to divide our efforts.

The Essence of Beauty

ONE THING THE Bible teaches very plainly is that Christ is the sum of all virtues and the essence of all beauty.

On this subject, modern Christians have a lot to learn. We have been cheated of this truth for the last half-century or more, the emphasis falling elsewhere. And we are always victims of the prevailing religious vogue. Whatever is getting the attention from our spiritual leaders is what we finally come to accept as orthodoxy in any given period of history. And right now we are definitely not hearing much about the loveliness of Jesus.

Christ is God shining through the personality of a man, and *shining unhindered*. His sacred humanity does not veil His divine beauty in any degree. The Christ who lived among men showed forth the nature of God as certainly as if He had still been with His Father in the preincarnate state.

There is no moral beauty but what Christ is the source of it. Every trait of lovely character we see in any believing man or woman is but an imperfect demonstration of how wonderful Jesus is. Even those moral beauties that appear to be "natural" to some people have their source in Him. For human goodness cannot exist apart from Christ.

They are but broken lights of Thee,
And Thou, O Christ, are more than they.

Some good Christians are afraid to give notice to
any lovely virtues which may appear here and
there among God's people lest they detract from
the glory of Christ. Such timidity is understand-
able, but uncalled for. If we know to begin with that
all goodness is from Christ, that all sweetness, all
holiness, all loveliness are out of Him and from
Him and in Him, we will not hesitate to recognize
moral excellence wherever it may occur on this dark
planet. If a ray of holy light shines out from any
man's life, it must be because Christ is there shining in secret in a human breast, and we should be
quick to catch this dim glimpse of the Light of the
World again incarnated in a human being. The
glory of Christ will not suffer from this frank and
eager acknowledgment of virtue where we find it.

Because we are sentient beings, we must have
some love-motivation to keep us running. This fact
(on a lower level) is well known to everyone. God
knew this (for He made us) and gave us the supreme love-Object of the universe to fire our hearts
with holy passion. That Object is Jesus. The Christian faith may be summed up in the love for Jesus.
To love Him enough is to be sweetly and wonder-
fully free. To love Him as He should be loved is to
know at once complete release from religious forms
and traditions. It is to reach the goal of life even
here below.

CHAPTER

19

Free, but Not Independent

IT IS A DIFFICULT thing to do, yet very necessary that we find a place of complete spiritual freedom and loving dependence upon one another.

Here in the wide valley between two high and dangerous peaks is the broad dwelling of God's true and wise children.

The spirit of complete inward freedom is a precious heritage from the cross and should be treasured as one of life's most wonderful possessions. It is our privilege to be wholly free from evil habits, from superstition, from the fear of men, from the slavery of popular customs, from the necessity of pleasing the self-elected dictators of society. Such freedom is wondrously delightful, near to the joy of heaven itself.

Our Lord said, "And ye shall know the truth, and the truth shall make you free. . . . If the Son therefore shall make you free, ye shall be free indeed." The one whom the Son has set free is as free from others as if there were no others living in the world. He would walk with God in quiet inward liberty if no one else on earth were to go along with him.

Yet such a happy soul has no feeling of independence; he is deeply conscious that he is a member of a larger body of which Christ is the head, and he willingly acknowledges his indebtedness to all other Christians. He thanks God for every one of His children and is eager to learn from all of them. He is grateful for "holy men of God who spake as they were moved by the Holy Ghost," for translators, expositors, teachers, intercessors, hymnists, and he thankfully acknowledges the part they all had in ministering to his own life the liberating things of the free Spirit.

It is most important that this truth be grasped firmly and taught faithfully, for as long as we are in this mortal body, there will always be danger from one or the other of these two extremes, slavish dependence or arrogant independence. Some Christians (by far the majority) will accept a place of timid conformity and surrender themselves to the bondage of authority and custom. In all things religious they will become meek followers of popular trends within their own circle. Such as these have no vision of their own, no true convictions, no inward freedom. They are slaves of the religious machine; they know nothing of the liberty with which Christ has made us free.

The other extreme is found here and there among us, and while it never has as many followers as the cult of bondage, it is nevertheless quite well represented in orthodox circles. Its followers glorify freedom to a point where they deny their proper debt to fellow Christians and scorn the interdependence of the body. They are often contemptuous of spiritual authority, and they deny the right of Spirit-gifted men to exercise their gifts within the church. This breeds a kind of religious anarchy that is altogether unscriptural and, as might be expected, extremely injurious to the cause of true spirituality. Both extremes must be avoided. We must live in the paradox of happy dependent freedom.

CHAPTER

20

Convention or Crusade?

Such a fast hold does inertia have upon almost everything religious that it takes a powerful and sudden attack by determined forces to move anything. It takes something like a crusade to get anything done these days. The principle of *laissez faire* is so firmly implanted in all of us that something in the nature of an earthquake is needed to jar us loose and start us on the right way.

It is an illuminating experience to read the history of the great spiritual movements that have blessed the world over the last 2,000 years. Scarcely any of these began quietly; almost always they struck the earth with the suddenness of a cyclone. We have only to mention a few to prove our point: the ministry of John the Baptist, the appearance of Jesus Christ with His miracles, Pentecost, the Reformation, the Wesleyan revivals, the Great Awakening, revivals in Wales, in Korea, the strange and wonderful work under the Prophet Harris in Africa—the list is long.

These movements struck with the unexpectedness of lightning and found people without a defense against them. Methodism, for instance, moved with the speed of a forest fire and took on the character of a crusade. The spiritual certainty within the hearts of a select few became so white-hot that it set others on fire around it and started an unplanned movement toward a return to New Testament standards and the deeper things of the Spirit.

History shows another fact also. When the first heat of the originators of great movements had spent itself after their death, immediately another spirit entered and took over—it was the spirit of conventionalism. It retained the outward form of the original movement but lost all the inward heat. The movement ceased to move; its adherents gained popularity and lost power; the apocalyptic quality of its message disappeared; its new teachers set about to make its teaching acceptable to Christendom—and their success became at last their greatest tragedy.

It is a lamentable fact that the crusading spirit is almost wholly lost to the deeper life branches of the church. Modern crusaders are for the most part no more than high octane proselyters operating down on a level far below New Testament plateaus. They make all the noise and get all the notice, while hungry-hearted saints shake their heads in discouragement and wait for—what?

It Will Not Go Away

A DROLL BIT of advice sometimes given to persons who are being bothered by some disagreeable problem is, "Let it alone and it will go away by itself." While the words are usually intended to be humorous, they express, better than many more serious words would do, an unfortunate habit which is altogether too prevalent among us. It is the habit of neglecting spiritual questions in the vague hope that they will stop bothering us and go away of themselves.

We all come into the world with one tremendous question facing us, the question of our relation to the God from whose hand we came. None of the heavy problems propounded by philosophy can equal this one in vital significance and solemn meaning for the individual man. So important is it that it may properly be said that no other question really exists at all till this one has been settled. And it will not settle itself; it must be settled by each one of us personally and individually. If we ignore it, it will not go away. It will be there to haunt us in the last day we spend on earth, and it will be there to face us in the day of judgment when it is too late to do anything about it.

This question is not a philosophical one merely;

it is not even a theological one. It is strictly personal. The deceitful human heart would like only too well to involve it in the fog of doctrinal argument and thus rob it of its real meaning. That is a common way to deal with it, but it is never a satisfactory way. The question will come back again out of the fog to demand a true answer, that is, a moral answer.

Two questions are embraced within the one problem: What shall I do with my sin? and what shall I do with Jesus which is called Christ? In spite of every effort of the pseudo-learned world to dispose of the sin question, it remains still, a perennial heartache to the sons and daughters of Adam and Eve. It is one of those persistent pains that lies deep in the soul and never quite stops hurting. It just won't go away. The devil and the busy sons of men have sought throughout the centuries for something to make this problem go away. They have invented how many thousands of amusements, they have created innumerable pleasures to take the mind off its central woe; but nothing works. Sin is still the world's first problem.

The second question, What shall I do with Jesus? is the answer to the first one, because Jesus came to save men from their sins. Let us answer the second one rightly and the first one will be solved automatically. If we but come to Jesus with our sin upon us and without any hope except His mercy, we shall surely be delivered from the ancient curse. But remember, sin demands an answer. It won't just go away. It must be carried away by redeeming blood, and redeeming blood was never shed by any other lamb except the Lamb of God.

Who Is in Debt to Whom?

THE LIFE IDEAL was described by the apostle in the Book of Acts: "For David, after he had served his own generation by the will of God, fell on sleep."

We submit that it would be difficult, if not impossible, to improve upon this. It embraces the whole sphere of religion, appearing as it does in its three directions: God, the individual, society. Within that simple triangle all possible human activities are carried on. To each of us there can be but these three dimensions: God, myself, others. Beyond this we cannot go, nor should we even attempt to go. If we serve God according to His own will, and in doing so serve our generation, we shall have accomplished all that is possible for any human being.

David was smart enough to serve God and his generation before he fell asleep. To fall asleep before we have served our generation is nothing short of tragic. It is good to sleep at last, as all our honored fathers have done, but it is a moral calamity to sleep without having first labored to bless the world. No man has any right to die until he has put mankind in debt to him. No man has any moral right to lie down on the earth till he has wrought to take something of the earth out of the hearts of men, till he has helped to free men from the tyranny of that same earth and pointed them to that kingdom that will abide after the heavens and the earth are no more.

David's religion had social implications, but he was no mere do-gooder, no patcher-upper of the world's hurts. All his service was rendered according to the will of God. It was the divine quality in his ministry that made it immortal. Many good deeds may be done whose final effects will not be lasting. A sick man laboring to cure the ills of another sick man may be a moving sight, but it can hardly be a reassuring one, for both will die at last. But the service that can bring the healing touch of God into human life is infinitely to be preferred to any other. It is the will of God that brings eternity into human toil.

We should remember that if we are to serve our generation we must get at it right away, for our generation will not be around long. Isaac Watts wrote:

> *Time, like an ever rolling stream*
> *Bears all its sons away;*
> *They fly, forgotten, as a dream*
> *Dies at the opening day.*

We are all born in debt to the world, and that debt increases as we grow older. If we are wise in the Spirit, we shall see to it that we turn the tables and put the world in debt to us. This we can do only by serving our generation by the will of God before it is too late.

True Service

A NY SERIOUS-MINDED CHRISTIAN may at some time find himself wondering whether the service he is giving to God is the best it could be. He may even have times of doubting, and fear that his toil is fruitless and his life empty.

This is not as bad as it sounds, and may actually prove to be an excellent thing for him—if he knows how to use it.

Christian service, like every other phase of religion, can become a very hollow affair. The church has marked out certain work and approved it as service acceptable to God, and for the most part the church has been right. But it should be kept in mind that it is not the kind or quantity of work that makes it true service—it is the *quality*.

Before the judgment seat of Christ, very little will be heard of numbers or size; moral quality is about all that will matter then. If we are wise we will give attention now to the quality of our service; it is obvious that it will be too late to do anything about it when the service is ended and the account rendered up.

The great weight of exhortation these days is in the direction of zeal and activity. "Let's get going" is the favorite watchword for gospel workers, with the result that everyone feels ashamed to sit down and think. But it will pay to do it, nevertheless.

It would be a shock to most of us to learn just what God thinks of our breathless activity, and a greater shock to many to find out the true quality of our service as God sees it. For not all religious activity is accepted of God, not even when it appears to produce results and get things done. The Lord seeth not as man seeth.

Christian service, to be accepted of God, must be fresh and sincere. Whatever is done out of habit is not approved; anything done in a perfunctory manner is below the level of quality expected of us. The careless song, the sermon preached for no higher reason than because it is Sunday again, the tithe tossed into the plate, the testimony given because it seems the thing to do—not one of these will stand up under the searching eyes of God.

In Christian service *motive* is everything, for it is motive that gives to every moral act its final quality.

Faith or Superstition

BETWEEN FAITH AND superstition there is a great gulf fixed. They are as unlike as light and dark and as far apart as heaven and hell.

Yet superstition may have every appearance of faith and may deceive us if we do not stay on the alert. Nor is this anything to wonder at, seeing that in every department of life there are opposites which appear alike to the careless observer. Even nature itself provides examples of this. The toadstool, for instance, looks so much like a mushroom that it takes a sharp eye to distinguish one from the other; yet one is an agent of death and the other a safe and nourishing food.

How then can we tell who is a true believer and who a victim of superstition? How can we know that we are engaged with reality and not simply imagining things? For without doubt there have been sincere men and women who have communed with unreality and found comfort in things wholly imaginary.

The problem is not simple but neither is it insoluble. If we will take the time to examine our own experience with due modesty and in the light of revealed truth, we may surely find our way around in this region of the soul.

Faith differs from superstition in its ground of hope. Faith rests upon character, specifically the character of God. A word is only as good as the character of the one who uttered it. Superstition counts upon a word, a text, and never thinks back of the text to the one who gave it. For the superstitious man there is a magic power in a word quite apart from the one who spoke it. The very word is magical and has only to be spoken under the right circumstances to be effective; morality or character have no place in this scheme of things. Words only count there. This in its various manifestations is a sure mark of superstition.

Even in some Christian circles this ill-grounded trust in sounds and symbols is encountered all too frequently. Some believers, for instance, fear to speak the name of Jesus apart from the titles which accompany it. They dare not say "Jesus," but must always say "the Lord Jesus Christ," regardless of the circumstances. Obviously they believe that God is concerned with the protocol of word arrangement and will be displeased if the order is broken. Such words as *amen, hallelujah, glory* and others of like sacred association are repeated endlessly and meaninglessly in the apparent belief that they have in them some strange power for good. This *can* be no more than high-grade magic. It will pay us to search our own hearts thoroughly to discover just why we use these words.

Any sound religious experience must begin with a proper conception of the nature of God. The terrible power of idolatry for evil lies in its unworthy conception of the character of the Supreme Being. Indeed it may be said without qualification that all religious experience that incorporates in itself low or ignoble ideas of God is in essence superstitious.

The god of superstition is an irresponsible god, arbitrary and without character. The superstitious person must constantly try to outwit him or placate him or catch him with words and force a favor out of him. But such a person is never at peace because he is never sure of anything. His hope is fugitive and skittish. There is no trustworthy being back of his faith; there are only words.

True faith does not rest upon texts alone but upon God who wrote the text. The word is an expression of the character of God and is exactly as good as that character, no more and no less.

The free man in Christ has been delivered from the "tyranny of words." He has gone beyond the word to God Himself and has found there his true fatherland and everlasting home. He can no longer be intimidated by the little slave-men who threaten him with punishment if he fails to repeat this religious phrase or mutter that sacred word. He has discovered the true ground of religious hope—the character of God. To such a man the Scriptures are the very words of God, meaningless apart from Him but altogether glorious when understood as the verbal expression of His holy being.

The Logic of the Incarnation

PROBABLY NO OTHER doctrine in the entire Word of God carries in it greater difficulties than the doctrine of the Incarnation. Paul called it the "mystery of godliness," and later writers either passed over its difficulties without trying to explain them or else involved the whole thing in a maze of explanations that offered little real help to an understanding of it. And we can easily see why this is so.

The Incarnation brings to us the essential mystery of being. It touches almost every phase of human thought and makes demands upon philosophy and metaphysics, as well as upon theology. The great doctors have felt this deep mystery whenever they have come to the consideration of the subject and have tiptoed along the borders of it with deepest reverence. That is proper and right; such an attitude well becomes us who are but dust and ashes.

At the risk of being charged with inexcusable boldness, we venture the assertion that while the Incarnation is mysterious, it is not illogical or contrary to reason. We would not presume to settle with a pen stroke those profound and awful mysteries which have stilled the voices of the ages and brought men and angels to their knees in worship; but we would dare to say that in our opinion the act of becoming man was altogether reasonable from God's standpoint. It placed no strain upon the divine nature and admitted into the scheme of God nothing unnatural or inconsistent. The reasons for so believing are these:

Man was originally made in the image of God. "God created man; in the likeness of God made he him." This is a cardinal doctrine of the Christian faith. It is not necessary to understand all that is included in this doctrine, for even here we run into some real theological problems. But faith can soar where reason can never climb, and it is only necessary that we believe the truth. Its power over us depends upon our believing it, not upon our understanding it. The fact is all that matters: man was made in the image of God.

Now, if man was made in the image of God, then God must certainly carry something of the image of man. (That sin has marred the image and introduced a foreign and destructive element into human nature does not detract from the force of the argument.) If a boy looks like his father it must surely follow that the father must look like the boy. Somewhere within man's nature, twisted and deformed as it may be, there is godlikeness. This will not be seriously questioned by anyone who knows his Bible. No student of Christian theology would deny this as a fact, though he might reject the conclusions we draw from the fact.

If in the infinite condescension of God, mankind was made with a nature somewhat like its creator, then is it not reasonable that God could clothe Himself with human nature in the mystery of incarnation? and all within the framework of easy possibility without the embarrassment of uniting things unlike each other?

When the ancient Word stood up in human flesh, He felt at home. He was not out of His element, for had He not heard the Father say, "Let us make man in our image, after our likeness"? There was no jar, no wrench caused by the forced union of dissimilar natures.

It is our humble opinion that the "exile" element in the earthly experience of our Lord has been greatly overplayed. That He was sad and lonely and far from home, a stranger in a strange land, is an idea that has grown up around the beautiful and simple fact, but it is not necessarily a part of the fact. So far as we can recall there is nothing in the record to give the impression that His presence in human flesh was an unnatural or painful experience. He happily called Himself "the Son of man," not an exile among men.

All this is not to attempt to take away from the valid mystery that surrounds the Incarnation or to lessen the awe with which we contemplate the wonder of the Word becoming flesh to dwell among us. It is rather to clear away unauthorized notions and give the beauty of the Incarnation a chance to make its own impression upon us. That impression will be deep enough without our adding anything to it.

Battles Are Won Before They Are Fought

THE WHOLE BIBLE and all past history unite to teach that battles are always won before the armies take the field. The critical moment for any army is not the day it engages the foe in actual combat; it is the day before or the month before or the year before.

The critical time for a singer is not the tense moment when he or she steps out to face a waiting audience. If the song has not been a success before that time, it will be no success then. Every musical triumph is the result of years of discipline and practice and hard work. Let a young singer imagine he can skip the tough preparation and he will soon be forgotten. He may get by for a little while on enthusiasm, personality and good looks, but the lack of foundation work will tell before long, and the public will pass him by for someone who is willing to pay the price it costs to win.

The pugilist must win his fight weeks before he steps into the ring or he will lose it. The farmer must prepare his field weeks before he plants it, or the resultant crop will be a failure. And with all of life the same rule holds. Preparation is vital. The rule is, prepare or fail. Luck and bluster will do for a while, but the law will catch up with us sooner or later, usually sooner.

It is an old saying that the wars of England were won on the playing fields of Eton. The experience of hard training, tough competition and sportsmanship gained in their school years prepared the young men for real war when it came. Again that rule holds for all of us everywhere, even up on the high levels of spiritual warfare.

It did not take Moses long to lead the children of Israel out through the Red Sea to deliverance and freedom; but his fittedness to lead them out was the result of years of hard discipline. It took David only a few minutes to dispose of Goliath; but he had beaten the giant long before in the person of the lion and the bear. Elijah faced a sulking King Ahab and stared him down in the name of Jehovah, but we must remember that his courage to stand before kings was the result of years spent in standing before the King of kings. Christ stood silent in the presence of Pilate and for our sake went calmly out to die. He could endure the anguish of the cross because He had suffered the pains of Gethsemane the night before; there was a direct relationship between the two experiences. One served as a preparation for the other.

The converse of this is true also. Battles are never lost the day they are fought. They are lost the day or the year before; the results merely become manifest when the armies meet. If we were wise enough, we could predict without fail the outcome of any battle, for the law of causation determines it always.

Lot fled from Sodom with the tattered remnant of his family and left all his property behind to perish in the flames, but his loss did not occur the night he escaped the burning city; it occurred the day he lifted up his eyes and saw all the well-watered plains of Jordan and coveted them. On a certain night Judas betrayed Christ with a kiss, but his tragic downfall did not take place that night; it only became evident. For months he had been undermining his own soul by filching from the meager funds entrusted to his care. He had gotten himself ready for the kind of death he died by the kind of life he had lived. His betrayal and suicide might have been accurately predicted by anyone who could have known what had been going on inside him during the days before the betrayal.

Preparation is vital. Let this be noted by everyone. We can seek God today and get prepared to meet temptation tomorrow; but if we meet the enemy without first having met God, the outcome is not conjectural; the issue is already decided. We can only lose.

We do well to imitate the ant who takes advantage of the summer to get ready for the winter.

CHAPTER

27

We Need the Spirit's Gifts

THE TASK OF the church is too great for any one person to compass and too varied for the skill of any one person to accomplish.

God has met this difficulty by dividing the task and giving to every man gifts that enable him to do his part. By distributing the work, He lightens the burden for all and makes possible the smooth carrying out of His purposes among men. That is undoubtedly the reason behind the gifts of the Spirit given to the various members of the Christian community. Here, as elsewhere, the manifold wisdom of God is revealed.

Not all men can sing; at least not all men can sing well enough to be heard in public. Only a limited number are called to preach. Real teachers are scarce because the gift which enables a Christian to teach is not given to many. Even the humbler gifts, such as "helps" and "governments," are given to relatively few. The gift of the evangelist is not given to all, or the pastor's gift or the gift of wisdom. Blessed is the man who knows his gift and who seeks to exercise it toward the other members of the body of Christ as a "good steward of the manifold grace of God."

The time is more than ripe for a rethinking of the

whole matter of spiritual gifts within the church of Christ. The subject has fallen into the hands of people for the most part extreme and irresponsible and has become associated with fanaticism in its various forms. This is a huge misfortune and is causing tremendous loss to the work of spiritual Christianity in our times.

Prejudices pro and con make the consideration of this subject extremely difficult, but its neglect is costing us more than we should be willing to pay. A revival of true New Testament Christianity must surely bring with it a manifestation of spiritual gifts. Anything short of it will create a just suspicion that the revival is something short of scriptural.

Let's Deal with Life at Its Root

ALL LIFE IS at root spiritual. God is spirit, and since He is the Cause and Origin of everything, it follows that everything originally came out of spirit. Matter may indeed be only the objectification of spirit. It is interesting to learn that modern science comes pretty close to teaching just that today.

It is not necessary, however, to understand the philosophical ground for this belief (if such ground exists); it is enough to believe the Scriptures, and they make it very clear that a human being is essentially a spirit clothed in a body, and that the inner life is the key to all the rest of the life. The whole Bible magnifies the inner and eternal part of man and lays correspondingly lighter emphasis upon the external and temporal.

Paul sang his ringing song of victory over this world, a song he could sing with all those who "look not at the things which are seen, but at the things which are not seen: for the things which are seen are temporal; but the things which are not seen are eternal" (2 Corinthians 4:18). Indeed it may be truthfully said that everything of lasting value in the Christian life is unseen and eternal. Things seen are of little real significance in the light of God's presence. He pays small attention to the beauty of a woman or the strength of a man. With Him the heart is all that matters. The rest of the life comes into notice only because it represents the dwelling place of the inner eternal being.

The solution to life's problems is spiritual because the essence of life is spiritual. It is astonishing how many difficulties clear up without any effort when the inner life gets straightened out. If half the time we spend trying to fix up outward things were spent in getting our hearts right, we would be delighted with the result. Strange as it may seem, harmony within our own hearts depends mostly upon our getting into harmony with God. Morning comes not by our pushing out the darkness but by waiting for the coming of the sun.

Church difficulties are spiritual also and admit of a spiritual answer. Whatever may be wrong in the life of any church may be cleared up by recognizing the quality of the trouble and dealing with it at the root. Prayer, humility and a generous application of the Spirit of Christ will cure just about any disease in the body of believers. Yet this is usually the last thing we think about when difficulties arise. We often attempt to cure spiritual ills with carnal medicines, and the results are more than disappointing.

Faith Is a Continuous Act

THE BOOK OF Acts lays strong emphasis upon steadfastness in the faith, as do the Pauline epistles and the Book of Hebrews. Obviously the apostles conceived the Christian life to be a long tough journey, requiring a lot of faith and determination but ending in glory at last.

Neither Christ nor His apostles taught the once-for-all finality of the act of believing so popular among us today. The whole build-up of the usual evangelistic meeting these days is toward the initial act of believing. Once a confession has been extracted from the seeker, a sense of victory seizes on everybody. It is as if a fish had been landed and safely stowed into the basket. The saving act has been performed, and there remains nothing more to be done. Not so taught the apostles or the faithful leaders of the church of God through the centuries.

Faith in Christ is not an act to be done and gotten over with as one might get inoculated against yellow fever or cholera. The repentant sinner's first act of believing in Christ for forgiveness and eternal life is the beginning of a continuous act of believing which lasts throughout life and for all eternity. "Then said Jesus to those Jews which believed on him, If ye continue in my word, then are ye my disciples indeed." These words accord perfectly with the exhortations of Barnabas to the Christians at Pisidia and Antioch: "That with purpose of heart they would cleave unto the Lord . . . confirming the souls of the disciples, and exhorting them to continue in the faith, and that we must through much tribulation enter into the kingdom of God."

We have heard of some churches that hold a service very early Sunday morning so the worshipers can get their religious duties over before going out to play golf the rest of the day. It gives them a comfortable feeling to know that their responsibilities toward God have been discharged with a minimum of inconvenience and without hindering in any way the fun of the day. We would be tempted to smile at this if we did not notice an uncomfortable parallel between that practice and the practice of getting our believing done early so that we might be free thereafter to walk as men.

The insurance policy aspect of salvation is very prominent in our times. We pay it up in advance (or allow the Lord to pay it) and from there on we rest in an accomplished fact. The urge to go on is almost wholly absent. This is not good, and it is surely not scriptural.

True faith is not an end; it is a means to an end. It is not a destination; it is a journey, and the initial act of believing in Christ is a gate leading into the long lane we are to travel with Christ for the rest of our earthly days. That journey is hard and tired, but it is wonderful also, and no one ever regretted the weariness when he came to the end of the road.

30

Deeds Are Seeds

EVERY MAN SOWS what he will later reap and reaps what he has previously sown. This is a law of life, says Paul, and we may as well know that we cannot beat it. God will not be mocked.

We are all sowing our own future, and the seeds we sow are the deeds we do. And, ironically enough, sometimes deeds we neglect to do or are afraid to do become seeds also and bring forth their harvest. For in the total scheme of things it often happens that deeds undone have as great power for good or evil as deeds actually performed.

The unbreakable link between harvest and seed was forged by the Lord God Himself at the creation. From Him went forth the word, "after his kind," and that word has linked together the seed and the harvest, the sowing and the reaping, from that day to this. Our today is bound to all our yesterdays, and our tomorrow will be the sum of our present and our past.

That is the fact, and we may make of it what we will. The sovereign God has permitted us to have a measure of conditional sovereignty, a mark of the divine image once given at the Creation and partially lost by the Fall.

We may sow to the flesh if we will. There will be

no interference from above. Thus to sow is our privilege—if we want to reap the harvest of corruption which must inevitably follow, a harvest no man in his right mind could deliberately choose. No, the snare lies in choosing the pleasures of sowing with the secret hope that in some way we can escape the sorrows of the reaping; but never since the beginning of the world has it been possible to separate the one from the other.

The way to deal with a law of God is to work along with it. By faith and obedience we can put every divine law to work for us. And the law of sowing and reaping may be brought to our service and made to toil for our everlasting good. So kind is God and so thoughtful of His creatures.

"He that soweth to the Spirit shall of the Spirit reap life everlasting." There it is, and we have but to submit *to* it to gain *from* it an everlasting reward. Deeds done in the Spirit, in obedience to Christ and with the purpose of bringing honor to the Triune God, are seeds of endless blessedness. The first gift of life is not by works, but by faith in the work of a sufficient Redeemer; but after the miracle of the new birth has been accomplished, the Christian to a large extent carries his future in his hands. If he denies himself and takes up his cross in meek obedience, his deeds will become seeds of life and everlasting glory. He may forget his deeds of love or think them small and useless, but God is not unmindful. He never forgets. The sweet harvest of a life well lived will be there to meet the sower after the toil is ended and the heat of the day is past.

Shadows versus Reality

B EHOLD, THY SERVANT," confessed Augustine concerning one period in his life; "behold, Thy servant, fleeing from his Lord, and obtaining a shadow."

"God is stupendously rich Reality," wrote von Hugel 1,500 years later, "the alone boundlessly rich Reality."

These sentences agree with and explain each other, and both accord with the teaching of Scripture and the facts of the creation. God is the only absolute Reality; all other reality is relative and contingent. While the things we know and experience day by day are real, they are not real in themselves, but only as God gives them existence. They could not continue to be should God withdraw His constant word of creation and leave them to themselves for even one short moment.

Here then is the rational ground for the Christian's insistence that God must be everything to us, that we must hold nothing dear except God. All other things are to be seen in relation to God and valued only as they are held in God and for God. All things are but shadows cast by the great Reality, God, and if we were to gain the whole world and miss God, we should have no more than a handful of shadows.

With this great eternal truth before His mind — the absolute reality of God as the central fact of existence — Christ taught the necessity of separation from the world and of complete consecration to God as the only way to escape the shadows and obtain those riches that cannot pass away.

The modern Christian who insists upon separation as a condition of true spirituality is not the old-fashioned narrow person he is currently declared to be. His religious philosophy is altogether sound and wholly in accord with the total sum of things in heaven and earth. God being who and what He is and things being what they are, complete consecration is the only way to peace for any of us.

The drift among Christians today is definitely away from this truth. More and more, our religious leaders are coming to place confidence in shadows and are teaching others to do the same. And just so far as shadows are accepted as real, the one great Reality is ignored. It is hard to think how a greater tragedy could possibly come upon us.

To the Spirit-filled Man Everything Is Spiritual

IT IS THE privilege of every Christian to live so fully in God that he never gets out of the experienced Presence for one moment.

When we have so learned to live in God and to experience His continual Presence, everything in our lives becomes spiritually significant. The old dividing line between the spiritual and the secular is removed, and every act becomes spiritual. What before had seemed mundane and nonspiritual now shines with a new light. God is found to be inhabiting our simplest acts as surely as our most lofty ones. All of life becomes good and acceptable to God through Jesus Christ our Lord.

A life lived in Christ becomes in the true sense a life of unceasing prayer. The whole life becomes a prayer: words are verbal prayers, thoughts become mental prayers, deeds become prayers in action and even sleep may be but unconscious prayer.

Psychology acknowledges a deep-down stratum of the mind which it calls the subconscious. It is that part which is in control during sleep and while we are under the power of an anesthetic. It *may* be the part of us that receives spiritual impressions first, becoming consciously aware of them only after they have first been received and registered in that mysterious depth of the mind which lies immediately below consciousness. Whether or not that is the correct explanation for things, it is still true that the whole mind may be placed so fully under the control of Christ that even sleep and forgetfulness work on our side to bless and help us in our practical waking lives. Whatever the explanation, the fact is known to every Spirit-filled Christian. We are only trying to state the familiar truth in less familiar language.

Let's Be Careful How We Use the Scriptures

THERE IS A naive assumption on the part of many that the Bible has about it some kind of magic power for good, so that merely to read it or quote it is profitable, regardless of the circumstances. This idea needs to be corrected.

Peter suggested that the writings of Paul might not always be profitable to everyone. ". . . Even as our beloved brother Paul also according to the wisdom given unto him hath written unto you; as also in all his epistles, speaking in them of these things; in which are some things hard to be understood, which they that are unlearned and unstable wrest, as they do also the other scriptures, unto their own destruction" (2 Peter 3: 15–16).

There is danger that the Word of God may become an opaque veil to hide God from us, and without doubt it sometimes is just that. The Scripture should be like the atmosphere, a transparent medium through which we look at the sun. When the atmosphere above us stops the light and allows us to *see it* instead of seeing *through it*, then its proper function is destroyed. So it is with the Word of God. When we so read the Bible as to make it an end rather than a medium through which we penetrate to the divine Person of God, it is no longer doing its proper work in us. Or otherwise stated, the Bible is a telescope through which we look at the "land that is very far off." When we become content with the telescope, it must surely fail us, for God never meant an instrument to take the place that belongs to Him alone; He never intended that a Book should substitute for the Living Word.

The threefold purpose of the Bible is to inform, to inspire faith and to secure obedience. Whenever it is used for any other purpose, it is used wrongly and may do actual injury. The Holy Scriptures will do us good only as we present an open mind to be taught, a tender heart to believe and a surrendered will to obey. If we do these things, then the written Word will surely become to us a transparent lens through which we may gaze upon the Triune God. And so to gaze in faith is to experience a bit of heaven here below.

We Are What We Are Anyway

Let not thy peace depend on the tongues of men," said the wise old Christian mystic, Thomas a Kempis; "for whether they judge well or ill, thou art not on that account other than thyself."

The desire to stand well with our fellow men is a natural one, and quite harmless up to a point, but when that desire becomes so all-consuming that we cannot be happy apart from the praises of men, it is no longer harmless, it is sinful in itself and injurious in its effects.

One of the first things a Christian should get used to is abuse. The sweetest soul ever to live in this world was subjected to an ever-increasing barrage of vile calumny during His walk among men; and if they so used the Master of the house, how can the servants hope to escape?

The only way to avoid evil tongues is to withdraw entirely from the society of men; and even then there might be those who would raise a meaningful eyebrow and suggest that perhaps after all we may have had a pretty good reason for getting under cover! To do nothing is to get abused for laziness, and to do anything is to get abused for not doing something else.

Was it not Voltaire who said that some people were like insects, they would never be noticed except that they sting? A traveler must make up his mind to go on regardless of the insects that make his trip miserable. They cannot stop a determined man; they can only make his journey unpleasant. So it is with the people who delight to swarm around the ears of God's servants as they move onward toward their appointed goal. We may all expect to be stung by our many fellow humans who appear to have dedicated themselves to the task of causing minor heartaches wherever they can as long as they can to as many people as possible. These misguided people cannot be escaped, they can only be endured.

One thing is certain, a Christian's standing before God does not depend upon his standing before men. A high reputation does not make a man dearer to God, nor does the tongue of the slanderer influence God's attitude toward His people in any way. He knows us each one, and we stand or fall in the light of His perfect knowledge.

Let us be sure that we are right with God and with men; after that there is nothing we can do except to "both hope and quietly wait for the salvation of the Lord." And by the indwelling power of the Holy Spirit, we may do our hoping and waiting in such a way that our enemies will be forced to admit that we have been with Jesus and learned of Him.

CHAPTER

35

God Can't Help Loving

MEISTER ECKHART SAID that God must love if He is to remain God. Were He to stop loving us He would lose His Godhead.

Such expressions as "if God is to remain God" and all others like them are in one sense ridiculous, for God can never cease to be God, nor can He lose anything that is Himself. The human mind, however, in its struggle to understand the impenetrable mysteries that surround the Person of God, is forced to think according to its own laws and to express itself in language that is in itself inaccurate, but which nevertheless represents an honest effort of the human heart to grasp the inconceivable. In saying that God must love us if He is to remain God, we are simply thinking human thoughts about God. It is the effort of the finite to contain the infinite, and while the thoughts are short of the mark, they are the best we are able to produce, we being what we are.

Eckhart was right in saying that God *must* love us. God being what He is, He has no choice. His love falls upon everything and everyone as the sun's rays light upon all the ten thousand objects on the face of the earth. The sun has no choice; it must shine on, whether it is shining upon a beautiful forest or a rubbish heap. The object upon which it shines has nothing to do with its shining. It shines because it is the sun.

God is love, so His loving is not something He may do nor not do at His will. Loving us is not an intermittent act or series of acts which God does in between other acts. His love flows steadily out upon the whole human race in an unbroken and continuous fullness. There is not a time, not a fraction of time, when God's love is not active toward us. It is as constant as the being of God, for it *is* the being of God in unforced, normal expression.

Everything that God does is done without effort or strain. He does all his acts with equal ease and tranquillity. We are often tempted to wonder how God could love us, but honest as this feeling is, it is nevertheless the result of a wrong way of looking at things. God does not love us because we are hard or easy to love; He loves us because He is God, not because we are good or bad or more attractive or less so. God's love is not drawn out of Him by its object; it flows out from God in a steady stream because He is love.

"God so loved the world," not because the world was lovable but because God is love. Christ did not die for us that God might love us; He died for us because God already loved us from everlasting. Love is not the result of redemption; it is the cause of it.

One question may demand to be answered: Does God love some people more than others? If not, what was meant by calling John "the disciple Jesus loved," as if to say that He loved John more than the rest? The answer is simple. John was more responsive to the love of Christ and could receive and enjoy it to a greater fullness. The divine love could operate toward this loving man with a joyous freedom not possible with others who had not his simplicity and faith.

The sunflower that turns its face to the sky all day long gets more sun than the violet that hides among the leaves. But the same sun shines in fullness upon both. God has no favorites, except as some of His children by their loving response make it possible for Him to shower more love upon them.

36

Jesus Is Victor!

T HE TWO MAJOR elements present in the Easter story are the *fact* and the *meaning* of the fact.

That Christ arose after He had been put to death by crucifixion is the fact; the true historicity of the event is too well established to require proof or even comment today. The meaning of that resurrection, however, must be rediscovered by each believing soul and by the church age after age till our Lord returns to earth again.

No one with the least trace of humility would attempt to state in one editorial the full significance of the resurrection of Christ. Were every meaning which that event carries written down, it might be said as it was said of the earthly activities of Christ, "Even the world itself could not contain the books that should be written."

One meaning attached to the resurrection is that Christ has conquered the enemies of mankind and guaranteed the final triumph of all true believers over every power of the devil. For the rescue of the lost race was effected only after a fight. Let us not allow our poetic imagination to run away with us. Easter is more than sunshine and lilies. It signifies the appearance again of our David who went into the field to meet the Goliath of sin and death in mortal combat. Christ came back to assure us that the victory had been won. Death and the devil had been done in by the only One who was capable of such a mighty act, Jesus the Son of God.

An old hymn states this for us in ecstatic language:

> The strife is o'er, the battle done;
> The victory of life is won;
> The song of triumph has begun—
> > Hallelujah!
>
> The powers of death have done their worst,
> But Christ their legions hath dispersed;
> Let shouts of holy joy outburst, —
> > Hallelujah!
>
> He brake the age-bound chains of hell;
> The bars from heaven's high portals fell;
> Let hymns of praise His triumph tell:
> > Hallelujah!

We might well spend the rest of the year reverently inquiring into the meanings of the resurrection. And probably the best method to pursue is to search for those meanings that touch us as individual Christians here and now. It is, of course, necessary to preserve the theology of the resurrection and to guard the truth well and carefully; but that is not enough. We must know what it means to us as pilgrims and strangers. That He "rose again the third day according to the Scriptures" is the biblical foundation for our faith in a risen Lord. But love and faith would go further; they would devoutly seek to experience the present riches of His Easter triumph.

Jesus is Victor! That is the truth His resurrection proclaims. Now it remains for us to allow Him to be victor in us, thus multiplying the glory of His triumph in the hearts of His trusting people.

The "Ground of the Soul"

IT IS THE teaching of Meister Eckhart that there is something far inside the mysterious depths of a human life which is unknown except as God and the individual know it. This he called the "ground" of the soul.

This "ground" is, according to Eckhart, the stuff which once received the image of God at creation. The lesser powers of the soul are the instruments through which this mysterious primal stuff makes itself felt in the world. These powers are imagination, reason, the faculty of speech and the creative powers which appear at full bloom in the artist and the poet and in varying degrees of brilliance in the commonalty of mankind.

In this far-in secret sanctuary, God reveals Himself to the individual as a "birth," bringing forth a new creation by the regenerating act of the Holy Spirit. Thus we receive from Christ the very nature of God (2 Peter 1:4) and are spiritually prepared for the full revelation of Christ in us, the hope of glory.

This would seem to be but a slightly different way of stating the truths taught by Paul in his inspired epistles. The apostle used the language of theology, or better still, he used the language of the Bible, but what he taught was not different from that taught by the man Eckhart. This great mystic theologian thought in terms of the psychology of his times, but when we make allowance for the difference of approach, the substance is the same. And a thoroughly Christian heart will understand the language of both.

The Holy Spirit never differs from Himself, and wherever He touches a human mind His sure marks are always present so plainly that there can be no mistaking them. Anyone familiar with the work of the French artist Millet will notice a similarity in everything he painted, as if the very breathing personality of the man had somehow gotten into the paint and onto the canvas. So the Holy Spirit teaches the same thing to everyone; however different the subjects may be from each other, the fine touch of the Spirit's hand may be detected on each one.

For this reason, Christian devotional books are very much alike no matter who may have written them or how widely divergent may have been the religious views of the authors. The masters of the inner life may at first appear to be far apart in some of their theological positions, but before he has read long, the delighted reader will discover the likenesses in the spirit of their teachings. They are talking about the same thing in their several ways and are as alike as various paintings by the same artist. The fragrance of the Rose of Sharon lingers over their pages; one face looks forth from the lattice and one voice is heard in the garden.

Because this is true, Eckhart's doctrine of "the ground of the soul" will be recognized as an old friend by the Spirit-taught Christian even though he has never before heard of Eckhart. He will find himself in familiar surroundings because he has walked there himself at other times and in different company.

However we may explain this mysterious "ground" within us, we will not have been long in the Christian way until we begin to experience it. We will find that we have within us a secret garden where no one can enter except ourself and God. Not only does no one else enter, no one else *can* enter. This secret inner chamber is the sacred trysting place for Christ and the believing soul; no one among all our dearest friends has the open sesame that will permit him to enter there. If God is shut out, then there can be only everlasting loneliness and numb despair.

Where God is not known in the inner shrine, the individual must try to compensate for his sense of aloneness in whatever way he can. Most persons rush away to the world to find companionship and surround themselves with every kind of diversionary activity. All devices for killing time, every shallow scheme for entertainment, are born out of this inner loneliness. It is a significant and revealing fact that such things have in these last days grown into billion dollar enterprises! So much will men pay to forget that they are a temple without a God, a garden where no voice is heard in the cool of the day.

The better minds among us, goaded by this subconscious loneliness, may, as Schopenhauer, become philosophers of despair or, as Byron and Hardy, poets of desperation and hopelessness. But no matter how brilliant the intellect, the lonely heart can never know peace. Until we find God through Christ, that inner "ground" will remain a kind of eternal thirst inside of us, and its voice, where that voice is recognized, will be a plea, an accusation, a thin plaintive cry deep within us asking for eternal life and restoration and God.

Driving with Our Brakes On

MANY CHRISTIANS LIVE like a man driving with his brakes on.

The car running with its brakes set is not standing still—not quite, but it is making a hard job out of an easy one. It is laboring unnecessarily, using more fuel than it should and sending up a stench from its overheated brake linings. And if the situation isn't corrected, it will not be going anywhere very long.

It is, of course, friction that retards the car's progress, for all brakes work by friction. The car is temporarily at odds with itself; one surface wants to revolve and another surface in contact with it wants to stand still. This clash of purposes sets up friction; and friction always wins at last. Nothing can continue to move if it is opposed by enough friction.

Even the most perfectly operated car cannot escape some resistance to its forward motion. There will always be gravity, air pressure and the unavoidable pressures of working parts that will tend to slow it down. But these are figured in and overcome by the steady application of energy to the wheels. It's the brakes that give a car a hard time.

Now all this would seem to be a parable of some kind.

The Christian need not expect to escape opposition. As long as Satan stands to resist the sons of God, as long as the world and the flesh remain, the believing man will meet opposition. Sometimes it will be sharp and obvious, but mostly it will be just the hidden and unsuspected friction set up by circumstances. No one need be anxious about this, however, for God has figured it in and made allowance for it. That kind of friction does little real harm. It will not retard progress much, and the very necessity of overcoming opposition will but add strength to the Christian's moral muscles.

But there is another kind of friction which retards spiritual progress and does real injury to the soul. It is the friction created by inward maladjustment.

Our Lord had this in mind when He spoke of the value of the "single eye," and James referred to the same thing when he told of the wavering man of double mind who was unstable in all his ways. While the heart is at cross-purposes with itself, there can be no inward harmony, only discord and carnal heat that slowly wear out the life.

One source of friction is resentfulness. To hold bad feeling against another is to put the brakes on; no matter how sincerely we desire to go on in the holy way, we are held back by the grinding of resentment within us. Morally resentment is static and will brake to a stop any soul that will harbor it. It is vitally important to remove the pressure that is checking forward motion. This we can do by for–

giving our enemies and taking pardon and cleansing from the Lord.

To name all the possible causes of inward friction would be to list the works of the flesh in their entirety. The flesh warreth against the spirit: that is, it seeks to stop the motions of the growing heart and bring it to a standstill. Or, failing that, it will put as much pressure as possible on the life and slow its progress as much as it can. The sad thing is that so many of us seem willing to let things go on that way. We "grovel here below," creeping forward painfully and at a snail's pace, when we might be racing unhindered toward the prize.

Let's check up on ourselves. Possibly we may need to take the brakes off.

Three Ways to Get What We Want

THE WORD WISH in its modern sense has little or no place in the Christian's vocabulary. The word occurs rarely in the Bible, and when it does it seldom means more than to will or desire.

It is hard to conceive of anything more completely futile than wishing. It is significant that wishing is done mostly by children and superstitious people. However sweet and innocent it may appear to see a child going through his little ritual of wishing, it can become something far from harmless when carried over into adult life. And even the child should be taught very early that wishing gets him nowhere.

The evil of the empty wish lies in the fact that the wisher is not adjusted to the will of God. He allows his desires to play over things that are entirely out of God's will for him and dreams of possessing what he well knows he should not have. Five minutes of this futile dreaming and he has lost the fine edge off his spiritual life. Should the act ripen into a habit, his Christian life may be seriously injured. The man soon comes to substitute mere longing for hard work, and unless he corrects his fault sharply, he will degenerate into a spineless dreamer of empty dreams.

Every desire should be brought to the test of God's will. If the desire is out of the will of God, it should be instantly dismissed as unworthy of us. To continue to long for something that is plainly out of the will of God for us is to prove how unreal our consecration actually is.

If, however, the desired object is legitimate and innocent, then there are three possible ways by which it may be obtained: one is to work for it, another is to pray for it and a third is to work and pray for it. These are clear methods by which God gives His good gifts to His people. They are not to be confused with each other and may be distinguished in practical living.

Some things are altogether out of the sphere of possibility for us, and yet altogether within God's gracious will for us. What to do? Prayer is the immediate answer. God has planned that we should go to Him for impossibilities when those impossibilities are a part of His eternal will for our highest good. Under such circumstances we should press our petitions upon Him with all the boldness and ardor of an obedient and trusting child. God loves such praying and has given every reason for us to believe that He will hear our prayer and in due time send the answer.

Other things can be had by the simple expedient of work. It is useless to ask God for something we could obtain with a bit of effort properly directed. No instructed Christian will waste his time praying for things that are within his own power to obtain. To do so is to deceive ourselves and make a farce of the whole concept of prayer. If work will get it for us, then work it is or we can go without it. God will not contribute to our delinquency by supplying us with gifts which we could get for ourselves but have done nothing to obtain.

But there is a third category consisting of desired objects which work alone can never secure. They lie far enough out of our reach that it will take something supernatural to get them for us, yet near enough that we must labor to obtain them. This adds up to *work and prayer*, and it will probably be found that the greatest majority of desired objects and objectives fall within this category. And this situation brings us close to God and makes us His co-laborers.

Whether it be a desire to open a closed field, win a hostile tribe, obtain a better job, build a new church, have a successful meeting, rear a family, get through school or do any one of an almost infinite number of legitimate things, the method is likely to be the twofold one of work and prayer. We might paraphrase the famous exhortation of Dr. Simpson and say that when faced with these borderline tasks which we must work at but which we can never do alone, the thing to do is to work as if we had it all to do and pray as if we expected God to do it all.

But wishing — let the vain dreamers and the builders of Spanish castles spend their time at it if they will. We know better than to waste our time and efforts at anything so useless.